This Book Belongs To

_____

Dedication

This book is dedicated to my children, Gabriella and Jordan. Your joy and laughter fill every holiday with warmth and inspire me every day. May this book bring happiness to all children and families, creating holiday memories to cherish forever.

Copyright © 2024 by Dr. Jessica Brown

GABBY CHOOSES A HEALTHY SNACK FOR SANTA

Authored by Dr. Jessica Brown

All rights reserved. No part of this book may be reproduced in any manner whatsoever without written permission.

Published by Boundless Butterfly Press, LLC New Jersey

Ebook ISBN: 978-1-956526-31-8

Paperback ISBN: 978-1-956526-29-5

Hardback ISBN: 978-1-956526-30-1

Library of Congress Control Number: 2024924351

Acknowledgements

A heartfelt thank you to My Belizean Gourmet Catering for providing healthy recipes and for your unwavering support throughout this journey. Your expertise and dedication to wholesome, delicious food have been a true inspiration.

For exceptional catering services, I highly recommend MBG Catering. Visit them at www.mybelizeangourmet.com.

Gabby Chooses A Healthy Snack for Santa

WRITTEN BY
DR. JESSICA BROWN

GABRIELLA &
JORDAN PIERRE-LOUIS

Message to Parents

As a parent, I understand how challenging it can be to promote healthy eating habits in children. With so many sugary snacks and processed foods readily available, it can be difficult to help kids develop a preference for nutritious options.

That's why I wrote Gabby Chooses A Healthy Snack for Santa. The story captures the magic of Christmas while highlighting the importance of a balanced diet. By introducing the five food groups in a fun and engaging way, I hope to spark conversations about healthy eating within your family.

Reading this book with your child(ren)is a wonderful way to start your own traditions while discussing the benefits of fruits, vegetables, and other nutritious foods. You can also try Gabby and Jordan's recipes to create healthy snack plates with your children, making food choices a fun and interactive activity.

Remember, small changes can make a big difference. Let's work together to nurture a generation that understands and embraces the importance of healthy eating.

If you need inspiration for recipes and ideas, my favorite resource is www.myplate.gov.

Wishing you and your family a happy and healthy holiday season!

Dr. Jessica Brown

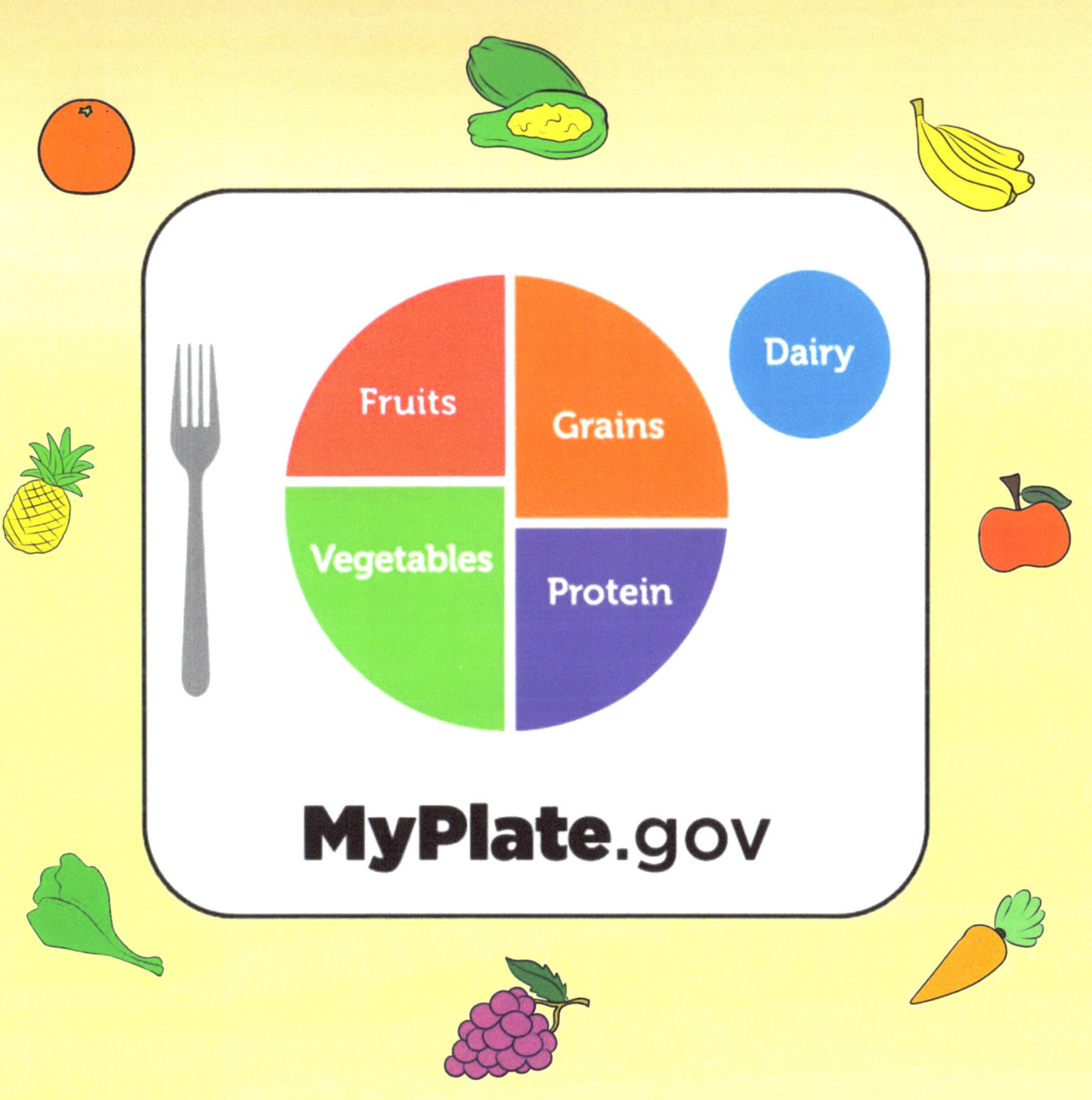

It was the night before Christmas, and Gabby and her little brother Jordan were filled with excitement. They had just finished decorating the house with twinkling lights and a tall Christmas tree.

First, they said a Christmas prayer, thanking God for their blessings. Afterward, they enjoyed a delicious dinner featuring their favorite foods: mac and cheese, collard greens, candied yams, and cornbread.

Every year, they left cookies and milk for Santa. But this year, Gabby had a new idea.

"Jordan, what if we leave Santa healthy snacks this year?" Gabby asked.

Jordan frowned. "Santa loves cookies. Why would we give him healthy snacks?"

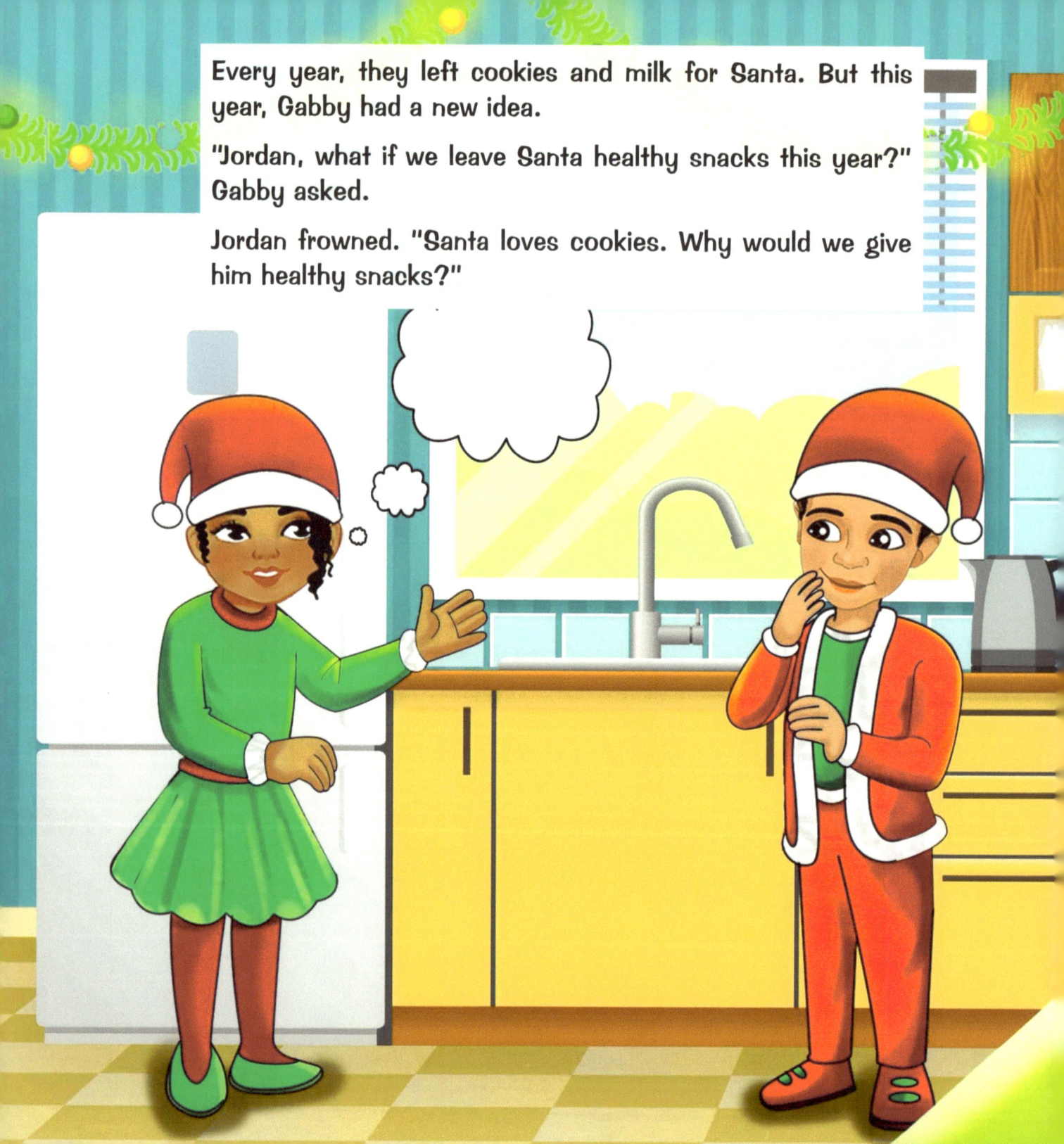

"Well," Gabby explained, "Santa gets cookies at every house. He might want something that helps him stay strong and full of energy. We can give him snacks from the five food groups: **fruits, vegetables, grains, protein,** and **dairy**."

Jordan thought about it. "Okay, but let's still leave a few cookies, just in case."

Gabby and Jordan got to work in the kitchen, making a **Healthy Snack Plate** for Santa.

"Let's start with **fruits**," Gabby said. She put some apples on a plate.

Then Jordan added some **carrot sticks** for the **vegetables**. "Santa can eat these, and we'll leave some for his reindeer, too!" Jordan said.

"For grains, we'll use the granola we made," Gabby said. They sprinkled it over a small bowl of yogurt with strawberries. "Yogurt is dairy and has calcium to help Santa's bones stay strong!" Jordan explained.

Finally, for protein, Jordan added a spoonful of **peanut butter** to dip the apple slices in. "This will give Santa energy to keep going all night!" he said.

Gabby and Jordan set the plate near the Christmas tree and wrote a letter for Santa.

Gabby and Jordan went to bed and were so excited for Christmas Day.

Up at the **North Pole**, Santa was getting ready for his big night of delivering presents. Soon, he was flying across the sky in his sleigh with his reindeer. Halfway through delivering presents, Santa started to feel tired from all the cookies left for him.

When Santa arrived at Gabby and Jordan's house, he smiled as he saw the plate of healthy snacks. "Healthy snacks from the five food groups? What a great idea!" said Santa.

Santa dipped an apple into the peanut butter. "Delicious!" he said, feeling refreshed. He ate the yogurt and granola, then nibbled on a carrot stick. "This is perfect!" he added, feeling strong and ready to continue his journey.

Before leaving, Santa wrote a letter for Gabby and Jordan.

Dear Gabby and Jordan,
Thank you for the healthy snacks! This will give me lots of energy to finish delivering presents. Eating from the five food groups helps me stay strong!
Merry Christmas,
Santa

The next morning, Gabby and Jordan rushed downstairs. They were so happy when they saw Santa's letter and the empty healthy snack plate!

"Gabby, Santa ate the healthy snacks and did not eat any of the cookies!" Jordan said with a grin.

Gabby smiled. "I told you! Even Santa needs healthy food to stay strong."

From then on, leaving healthy snacks for Santa became a new family tradition. Every year, they made sure to give Santa something from the five food groups, helping him stay energized for his long night of delivering presents.

Santa's Snack Trees

Servings: 6
Prep Time: 15 minutes
Total time: 15 minutes

 6 pita bread, cut into 4-5 triangles each

8 oz cream cheese, at room temperature

4) Serve:

Arrange the pita trees on a festive platter and serve immediately.

munch munch!

3) Add the Pretzel Tree Truck:

Gently press a pretzel stick into the bottom edge of each pita triangle to act as the "tree trunk"

1 tablespoon fresh dill, finely chopped

1 tablespoon fresh cilantro, finely chopped

1 tablespoon lemon juice

1 tablespoon scallion, finely chopped

2) Assemble the Pita Trees:

- Take each pita triangle and spread about 1-2 teaspoons of the herbed cream cheese mixture on top, covering the surface.

- Decorate a few pieces of vegetables over the cream cheese. Pretend they are holiday decorations.

1/4 cup of small diced vegetables (cucumber, red or green bell pepper)

24-30 pretzel sticks (1 per pita triangle)

stir stir!

1) Prepare the Herbed Cream Cheese Spread:

In a medium bowl, mix together the cream cheese, cilantro, scallion, dill, and lemon juice. Stir until smooth and well combined.

spread spread!

Jingle Berry Delight

1) Prepare the Mint Yogurt Mixture:

2 cups of yogurt

1 cup of sliced strawberries

In a medium bowl, combine the vanilla Greek yogurt with chopped mint leaves. Add the green food coloring and stir until the yogurt is evenly tinted and speckled with mint.

Servings: 4
Prep Time: 15 minutes
Total Time: 15 minutes

6-8 fresh chopped mint leaves

1 teaspoon of Green food coloring

1 cup of raspberries

mix mix!

yum yum!!

chill for up to an hour

Layer of raspberries

1/2 tablespoons of granola

1/4 cup of mint yogurt mixture

repeat repeat!!

2) Assemble the Parfaits:

In each serving glass, layer as follows:

3) For Garnishing:

Top each parfait with extra granola, a few berries, and a sprig of fresh mint for a festive touch.

peppermint candies

Top with more fresh berries!

Blueberries

Fresh mint

Author's Bio

Dr. Jessica Brown is a certified nurse practitioner, professor, and mother of two. She created *The Gabby Series* to promote health and wellness while highlighting diverse voices in children's literature. *Gabby Chooses a Healthy Snack for Santa* is the third book in this engaging series. Dr. Brown inspires positive change through her writing and her publishing company, Boundless Butterfly Press.

Learn more about her work and upcoming releases at
https://www.boundlessbutterflypress.com

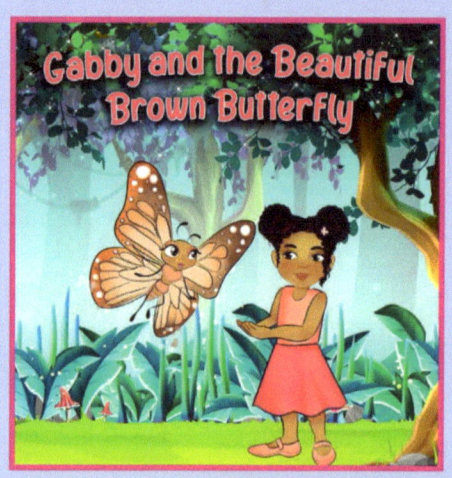
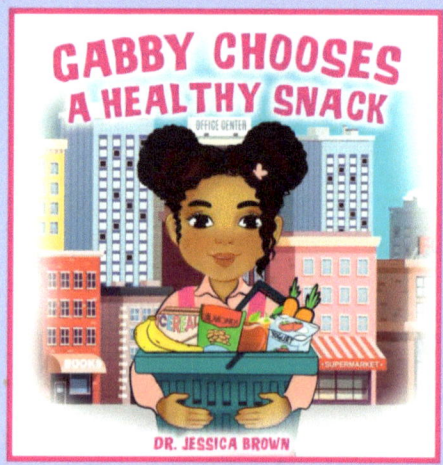
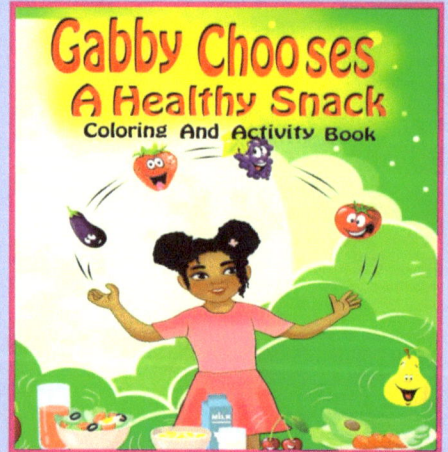
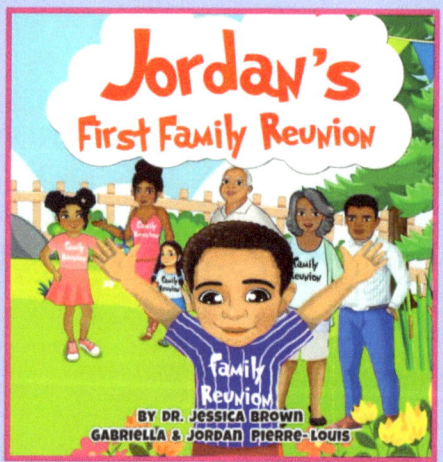

www.ingramcontent.com/pod-product-compliance
Lightning Source LLC
Chambersburg PA
CBHW041405010526
44107CB00015B/1085